A Month of

Stories

Creative Writing for Reluctant

Writers

Amanda J Harrington

author of the Creative Writing for Kids series

& Creative Comprehensions

Contents

4

Introduction

Have you ever wondered how to help your child write more stories? This book is a gentle introduction to story writing, with simple exercises that are entertaining and make creative writing fun.

Children who struggle with writing will not be put off as all the exercises give some help to get them started, while leaving enough room for each story to turn out differently. The mini-stories, included as examples, also give your child **reading practice** and the process of reading the instructions, as well as writing their own stories, is valuable experience for less confident readers.

Don't be afraid to try **new ways to create stories**, using conversation and pictures as well as writing about them. Help your child enjoy creative writing, at the same time as encouraging them to follow guidelines so that they become used to writing stories when asked, like at school.

The book contains 31 story ideas, one for every day of the month (and a few extra for February!). The exercises alternate between **story scenarios**, described in words and **story starters**, using mainly images. There is no need to follow the order in the book, let your child choose one they like and start with that.

For the written scenarios, I have included **example stories** so children can see how they might write their own. I have deliberately kept my examples short as this gives children reassurance that their own stories don't have to be very long, as well as making them feel good if they write more than I did!

The story starters with pictures all have the same

instructions, to use the picture to write a story, while each has a title that is designed to **spark ideas**. Some children who struggle with creative writing find it easier to use pictures to kick-start their imagination, so don't be afraid to let them concentrate on these exercises if they find them more attractive.

This book is intended to be **a taster for creative writing**, to encourage children to have fun and relax and to help them see how much they can achieve with a few ideas and some time to write. The story starters within this book are simple enough for children to use on their own and are a good foundation before moving on to the **Creative Writing for Kids** series.

As with most of my creative writing books, these exercises are aimed at children aged between 7-14, but are suitable for other ages depending on ability and parental help.

Amanda J Harrington

18/04/2013

Don't stomp on me!

Who would say this and why? Think of a small story to go with this sentence.

Here is my story:

Bobby the puppy was sick of being small. Every time he came out of bed, he had to run about so that people wouldn't stomp on him. He couldn't wait to be big and strong like his mother. Then he might just stomp on them and see how *they* liked it!

Horror!

Write a story based on this picture, about anything you like!

I hate you!

Oh dear, have you ever said this? Or has someone said it to you?

Imagine a story where someone says this and see if you can work out why.

Here is my story:

"I hate you!" my sister screamed at the top of her voice. I stood, trying not to laugh as her face turned pink. It was good her face was pink because now it matched her hair. I had swapped her shampoo for bright pink hair dye and now she had a really great new style…at least I liked it!

I don't care!

Write a story based on this picture, about anything

you like!

Maria is funny

You want to be best friends with the new girl at school. Her name is Maria and she is really funny. She knows lots of jokes and says silly things in class too.

How are you going to become friends with Maria? Write a story about what happens.

Here is my story:

Everyone was laughing at something Maria had just said. She was never going to notice me, I had to do something really good to get her attention.

I climbed onto the teacher's desk, put my arms in the air and shouted,

"Look, Maria, I'm a penguin!"

I did my special penguin walk across the desk,

knocking off books and a pencil sharpener. When I got

to the other end, I did a funny waddle and shouted,

"Here I jump into the sea!"

As I jumped, Miss walked through the door…

I'm the best!

Write a story based on this picture, about anything you like!

Find it, quick!

If anyone finds out you lost Grandma's door key,
you'll be in big trouble! You were meant to be looking
after it while she went to the hairdresser. Now it's gone
and Grandma and Mum are walking up to the front door.

Write a story about what happens next.

Here is my story:

Grandma was always losing things and forgetting
what she had done with them. Maybe I could pretend she
never gave me the key? Then she would be in trouble
instead of me?

I felt a bit guilty but I didn't want to be in trouble.

I waited for them to come in, trying to look nice and
good. As I got ready to lie, the dog ran past with the key

in his mouth.

Grandma and Mum looked at me, waiting for me to speak.

"Grandma!" I said, waving my arms, "Why did you give your key to the dog?!"

I don't like that!

Write a story based on this picture, about anything you like!

Be careful!

That was the last thing your Uncle Dan said to you as he gave you his watch.

Were you careful? Is his watch ok? Or did it have an accident?

Write about what happens when he comes back for his watch.

Here is my story:

I have no idea what happened but somehow that lovely, shiny watch turned into this little heap on my bedroom floor. I don't remember standing on it. I wonder if somebody else stood on it?

Later, when Uncle Dan has gone home, I look under the bed at the heap of watch pieces. I pushed them under right before he came in. I told him I'd lost his watch and he's waiting for me to find it.

Somehow, between now and tomorrow I have to learn how to fix watches. I'm sure it'll be fine, what could go wrong?

That's so funny!

Write a story based on this picture, about anything you like!

Yes, it *was* meant to be like that.

Isn't it horrible when you do a wonderful picture and someone is nasty about it?

This story is about what happens when Rebecca makes fun of your picture in front of everyone at school.

Write a story describing how you feel and what you do.

Here is my story:

Later, I went back into the classroom and took out all the pictures. I wanted to see if mine really was the worst in the class.

As I looked through them all, I realised there was

nothing wrong with my picture. It wasn't the best but it wasn't the worst either. Why did people have to be so mean?

When I came to Rebecca's picture, I held my breath. It was awful. You couldn't even tell it was meant to be a hippo. Why did she say those things about my picture when hers was so bad?

Shaking my head, I put them all back. I wasn't going to let her upset me anymore.

Feeling happier, I went back outside to play.

I'm not smiling!

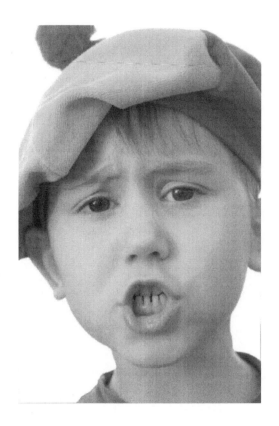

Write a story based on this picture, about anything you like!

Tumble-down

This can mean that something is broken, like a little old cottage, or it means when you, or something else, falls down, like when you roll down a hill.

Choose one of these meanings and write about it in a story.

Here is my story:

Every time I go to the seaside, I play tumble-down on the little hill next to the beach. Sometimes I take an old piece of cardboard and slide down, instead of tumbling. If my brothers go with me, we have tumble races down the hill. Usually, they win because they don't care if they hurt themselves.

Fairytale

Write a story based on this picture, about anything you like!

It's brown...

As a surprise, your dad has decorated your bedroom: in **brown**. Everything is brown, the walls, the new carpet, the new covers on the bed. Even the TV has been painted in dark brown paint to make it match.

What do you do?

Here is my story:

I can't believe I have to keep my bedroom like this! Dad says the paint and the carpet cost too much to change and he was sure I told him brown was my favourite colour. I did not! It's not fair, I have to put up with it and there's nothing I can do.

I have to wait until it needs decorating again before it can be changed and that could take years. Oh well, maybe I'll like it better in the morning? Or maybe, just to be nice, I'll wait until Dad goes out to work and I'll redecorate *his* room with the rest of the paint?

Now, wouldn't that be a good idea?

A strange day

Write a story based on this picture, about anything you like!

Here is the witch's house.

Write a short story using these words. Use your imagination to describe the house and, if she appears, the witch.

Here is my story:

We crept around the side of the house, determined to get a closer look. Quiet as could be, we had almost reached the back door when Greg jumped up, made a squealing noise and cried,

"Here is the witch's house!"

We all looked at him in horror. What if she found us? We were meant to be sneaking!

Before we had a chance to tell Greg off, the door of the house opened and a hand touched him on the shoulder.

It's all perfect

Write a story based on this picture, about anything you like!

My dog did it.

You're in big trouble so you blame the dog.

Do you get out of trouble again or make things worse? Can you really blame the dog for something you did?

Write a small story about what happens.

Here is my story:

We were both in trouble, me and Crispy. We sat in my room and looked at each other and the more Crispy looked at me, the worse I felt.

How could I blame poor Crispy for breaking the light? He can't even kick a football. I'm sure Mum knows it's me but she's sent Crispy to my room as well, so I know he's in trouble.

I should be really brave and tell her the truth. Then maybe Crispy won't stare at me anymore. It's almost like he knows what I've done.

Good friends, bad friends...

Write a story based on this picture, about anything you like!

What is that?

You get a present from Uncle Harry. It's a tiny wooden box and it rattles when you shake it. You can't get it open.

Write a story about what happens when you try to open the box. Do you find out what is inside? Is it something exciting or strange or is it just a normal box?

Here is my story:

I took the box to school and me and my friend Toby worked on it all break. We had just got the top loose when we had to go back in to class.

In the middle of the lesson, Mrs Clay stopped talking, looked at my school bag and pointed.

"What is that?!" she cried.

I looked and saw the box, tumbling slowly out of my bag. No, it wasn't tumbling, it was walking!

We all watched as the box hopped off my bag and onto the floor. Then it shot off under the desks and away.

Lazy days

Write a story based on this picture, about anything you like!

Don't go down there!

Write a story about not doing as you are told. You can be as naughty as you like, but include the words, 'Don't go down there!'

Here is my story:

Me and Erin were going to look in the cellar. It was cold and dark and there were cobwebs everywhere. Erin loved spiders and I loved adventure. We would find both down in the cellar.

We waited until we were alone, then opened the cellar door. As we went through, a voice shouted, "Don't go down there!"

We turned, but there was no one there…

I can't wait!

Write a story based on this picture, about anything you like!

Cats like...

What do you think cats like? Try to think of something that cats don't usually like and write about it.

Here is my story:

Custard likes pancakes. He doesn't mind if you cook them first or just give him the pancake batter. If I make pancakes, I have to put him out of the kitchen because if I don't, I'll suddenly find a small tabby cat, sitting too close to the frying pan, wondering if he can get his paw in there without burning himself.

Feeling funny

Write a story based on this picture, about anything you like!

My face is dirty.

You are all dressed up and on your best behaviour for your cousin's birthday party. You have to be super-good today because your cousin's family like everything to be nice and quiet and don't put up with anything silly.

Write about the party and fit in the words, 'My face is dirty,' anywhere you like.

Here is my story:

I can't wait to get home. Everyone is glaring at me and I haven't even done anything yet! All I did was look at the cake, I hardly even touched it.

I scratch my face and something comes off on my hand. My face is dirty, how did that happen? Then I realise it's not dirt, it's chocolate icing.

Oh no, now everyone will know I ate the cake!

Something Scary

Write a story based on this picture, about anything

you like!

Don't lift the lid!

You've been left alone with a giant box of chocolate biscuits. You're not allowed to have any until your Mum and Auntie come back in, but it's like the box is talking to you. You keep looking at the box, at the pictures of biscuits and can't wait for them to come back.

No one would notice if you just had one biscuit, would they? Your hand moves closer to the box. Your fingers start to feel along the edge. Then, just as you prise it open, a sound comes from the box.

What happens next?

Here is my story:

Suddenly, I'm inside the box! How did that happen? Did the box grow and swallow me up? Did I shrink?

I'm sitting on a chocolate cream biscuit (it smells great) and I can see a tiny bit of the room through a gap in the box lid.

Then I hear Mum and Aunty Jane coming in.

"Oh, lovely, let's have a biscuit!" Mum says and lifts the box lid.

Adventures

Write a story based on this picture, about anything you like!

Onions, tomatoes and pears!

Every time you open your mouth to say something, you talk about onions, tomatoes and pears. Think of a story to go around this and have fun!

Here is my story:

I tried not to say anything but couldn't hold it in any longer. Before I could stop myself, I shouted across the classroom:

"Onions are very good for you!"

I clapped a hand over my mouth, but it was too late. Miss Cleaver stared at me and said,

"I expect they are, now let's get on."

"Tomatoes are a fruit!" I yelled from behind my hand.

Everyone starting laughing as I put my head on the desk and tried to keep my mouth shut.

"Pears make my teeth ache…" I whispered to myself, wondering when this day would ever end.

For free chapters and resources, visit

www.thewishatree.com

Amanda J Harrington also writes the blog Crazy

Girl in an Aspie World, about being an adult with

aspergers. Her book, A Guide to your Aspie, is

available now on Amazon. For the blog, please visit

http://aspie-girl.blogspot.co.uk/

Printed in Great Britain
by Amazon.co.uk, Ltd.,
Marston Gate.